RAMBLINGS OF AN OLD MAN

Straight from the Heart (and a few from the hip)

By

William Arthur Nahmens

"Ramblings" is a collection of Poems and "Moral of the Story" and jokes by William Arthur Nahmens, as well as writings from others. It is divided into two sections. Part one is named "Straight from the Heart" and contains Poems either written from the Author's heart or have touched his heart in some way. Part two is a collection of either Humorous stories he has told(to make a point) or stories that just made him laugh along with some of his best (or worst, depending on your point of view) "Bad Dad/Grandpa jokes. His hope is that the reader will find something that either touches their heart or makes them laugh (or groan).

RAMBLINGS OF AN OLD MAN

I wonder who will read the ramblings of this old man

These pages where I have set pen to paper, bearing my soul

I have tried to express the pain of a heart that has lost at love

Feelings I've kept hidden, buried deep inside, afraid to let anyone
see

Still, some were written for others, who touched my heart and
life

While some were written from the depths of my broken Spirit or
heart

During the darkest of times, when I lost a loved one or a close
friend

Some of my Ramblings were written out of the joy of a child or
grandchild

Some were written out of love for a special family member of
friend

And then there are those "Bad Dad Jokes" and humorous stories I
have told

So, as you read these Ramblings from this old man, please tread
through lightly

Remembering, you are not just reading a book; you are looking
deep into my soul

I HOPE YOU ENJOY THE RAMBLINGS OF THIS OLD MAN

Dedication

In place of a dedication, I inserted this writing by Nakeia Homer.

It is a reminder to all who read this book that no matter what they may have gone through, are going through, or will face in the future, to just keep going. You can make it as long as you keep going. I know this writing has given me the strength to keep going many times when all I wanted to do was just quit.

May you never forget that
when it was hard, and you
were overwhelmed, and felt
afraid, and walked alone,
and felt invisible, and
didn't have the answers,
and couldn't see the way,
and wanted to give up....
you kept going.

Nakeia Homer

About the Author

William Arthur Nahmens is a United States Marine Corps Veteran. He served eight years, reaching the rank of Sergeant. His stories are a combination of personal experiences and stories told to him by others he has met over the years, sprinkled with just a touch of fiction (for added excitement). He is legally blind and spends most of his time writing poetry and stories about charters he has met during his life time. He loves spending time alone with his memories. His hope in writing is twofold. First, to tell others who have gone through similar experiences that it is to be human and show your emotions. Second, to give those who never served a glimpse of what Military life is like and offer them a chance to take a glimpse into the mind of a Marine. That glimpse can be both enlightening as well as freighting as you learn what it takes to become a Marine and what it means to be a Marine. The saying "Once a Marine. Always a Marine: is not just some mindless words strung together. It is a code every Marine lives by for the rest of their life.

PART ONE:
Straight from the Heart

SECTION ONE

DEATH AND DYING

HOW LONG IS A LIFETIME?
About the Poem

I wrote "How Long is a Lifetime" after the death of my friend Roger Angel. He was my friend all the way through school and even afterwards. I saw him just the day before he died. He was in the VA Hospital, and we were having some good laughs. I spoke to him the day he died; he was waiting to be discharged. He died as he was getting ready to leave the Hospital. Everyone was shocked by his sudden death. I heard people saying, "He was too young to die. He had a whole lifetime ahead of him." It made me wonder and ask the question, "Just how long is a lifetime." One thing I found out is that it is never long enough for those who are left behind. It matters not how long or short one's life is. It was never long enough. Just remember, we are not promised tomorrow; we are only promised today.

HOW LONG IS A LIFETIME?

"How long is a life time?" One often asks,

As long as morning dew on a rose pedal lasts.

Just as long as a snowflake in your palm will stay

As long as the last rays of sunlight take to fade away.

Life is never long enough, no matter what we think;

It is over faster than what it takes an eye to blink.

So, cherish each moment with loved ones spent;

Don't waste time on foolish arguments and desent.

That person you are with today may be gone tomorrow,

Leaving you with nothing more than guilt and sorrow.

A life time goes by much like a puff of smoke;

Disappearing as fast as a lightening bolt

So, when you ask yourself, "How long is a lifetime?"

Consider this: life is shorter than this last line.

William Arthur Nahmens

THAT SAD DAY
About the Poem

I wrote "That Sad Day" after my Uncle had died. I remember how, at the viewing, people were talking and laughing amongst themselves as my Aunt stood there at the closed casket, staring in disbelief. I remember wondering what I could do to ease her pain. I have always been the family comedian, but no joke could help her through this. Realizing there was nothing I could do our say to change things, I just stood off to the side (away from everyone else) and cried as I watched her standing there in numbing pain.

THAT SAD DAY

You locked afraid and lonely on that sad day,

I stood there looking, not knowing what to say.

I wanted to tell you that everything would be fine,

That you would heal if you just give it some time

On that day, I could not speak those words to you,

For even I did not believe them to be true.

I wanted to hold you and take all your pain,

But I knew any attempt would just be in vain.

And so I just stood in the shadows and wept,

Watching as you, your lonely vigil kept.

William Arthur Nahmens

THE EMPTY CHAIR
About the Poem

I wrote "The Empty Chair" For a former Classmate of mine, Kathy
Nelson/Nimtz (She gave me permission to use her name). Although I
was not real close to her in High School, I always thought she was a
very kind person. I saw her at our 50th Class Reunion, and she seemed
as kind as when she was in High School. She has a gentle and sweet
spirit about her. I wrote this after learning she lost her Step Dad (he
was almost 100 years old). She had been his and her Mother's
caregiver. Although it was a labor of love, I know how it can take a toll
on someone. It takes a special kind of person to do what she has done. I
wanted to somehow return just a small portion of the kindness she
always showed others.

THE EMPTY CHAIR

When you look and see the empty chair

Do not weep, for I am there

I am the shadow you see on your walls

I am the last ray of light as night falls

I am the wind that ruffles your hair;

I am the gentle breeze that brushes your cheek with care

I am that butterfly you chased through the meadow

At night, when you lay your head, I am your pillow

I am the unseen hand that dries your tears

I am the still, soft voice that calms your fears

So, when you look upon the empty chair

Give me a smile, for I am there.

William Arthur Nahmens

NEVER SURRENDER
About the Poem

I wrote "Never Surrender" as a promise to myself to keep fighting as long as I can. I will never give up or surrender to *ANYTHING*! I have spent most of my life-fighting something. Long before I became a Marine, I had the mentality to never quit or give in; the Marines put it into words and then into action. I never really gave this another thought (after being discharged from the Marines) until one day when I was talking to Arneetrice (One of the workers in the Low Vision Clinic at the VA). I mentioned this to her, and she said she was going to use this as one of her daily sayings: "I will NEVER surrender of my own free will, as long as I have the means to resist". I decided to make it into a poem. Thank you, Arneetrice, for the inspiration.

NEVER SURRENDER

I will never surrender my own freewill as long as I
have the means to resist

I learned this rule while in the Marines; every day,
they drilled my head with it

I have learned that what they meant for combat
actually applies to any war

In whatever battle I must fight, no matter what
hardship I must face or endure

Now, I find myself in the toughest battle of my life.
Cancer is a mighty foe

I will fight hard and as long I can; maybe I win, maybe
I lose, I don't know

To myself, this promise I make: win or lose, cancer
will know it has been in a fight

I refuse to just lay down and give up; I refuse to go
quietly into the dark of night

When others thought I was done or should give up
and quit, this line has brought me through:

"Never quit or surrender of my own free will as long I
am able to resist." This is what I will do

William Arthur Nahmens

MY RACE OF LIFE
About the Poem

I wrote "My Race of Life" as I looked back over the years at the many struggles I faced and the obstacles I had to overcome in my personal life. Obstacles that most people who know me know very little or nothing about. I thought about how people think I accomplished very little or overcame really nothing. My purpose here was to have others judge me and my life for me, just being me and NOT for what they thought I should be or should have done. Their life is theirs to judge, while My life is for me and God to judge.

MY RACE OF LIFE

When my race of life is run

Judge me for the things I have done

Judge me not by what you wanted to be

Just judge me for myself, me being me

Maybe to you, my accomplishments were small

To me, they were mighty, everyone standing tall

Some of which, to you, might seem like a small thing

But each was hard fought, and each left its sting

While some battles did knock me to the ground

I always got back up! For I refused to stay down

In looking back at all the things I have done

I have some regrets, yes; still, it was a great run

William Arthur Nahmens

LEAVING
About the Poem

I wrote "leaving" after finding out I had Cancer for the 3rd time. I had promised someone (after she lost some one very close to her) that I wouldn't leave. That was after getting cancer the 1st time. She had said (after finding out I had Cancer), "You'll leave me too, you'll see." I beat the cancer that time, so I told her, "See, I told you I wouldn't leave you." I never told her about the 2nd time. The 3rd time, there was no hiding it. She was once again back to doubting I would never leave. Now, I am fighting it again for the fourth time. I am deep in the battle, and it seems as though I will be unable to keep my promise to her. I only ask for her forgiveness for breaking my promise never to leave her alone. I am so sorry I couldn't stay.

LEAVING

Remember when I promised I would never leave

How you doubted me; you said you did not believe

Now, the time has come when I must go

And you will say, "See, I told you so."

The time of my leaving is not my choosing

My battle is with cancer, and I am losing

I fought long and hard, trying not to leave

Fighting so you wouldn't be left alone to grieve

With each new day, I began the battle-anew

Fighting with all my strength, doing all I could do

All the time keeping, upon my face, a painted-on smile

Fighting and smiling to hide the pain inside all the while.

Keeping my fears and my pain buried deep inside

Knowing that, if you knew, you would have cried

So please forgive me and try to believe

I fought long and hard, trying not to leave

William Arthur Nahmens

THE DAY DAD DIED
About the Poem

I wrote "THE DAY DAD DIED" as a tribute to my Father. I wasn't there when he passed away. I was many miles away. I planned to get there, but time ran out before I could. Just about a week before, I saw him, but I barely spoke to him. I was angry about an argument we had a couple of weeks before that. He was screaming at me, so I ended it by saying, "I really don't want to talk to you anymore." Now, I live with those final words every day of my life, regretting them and unable to take them back or apologize to him for saying them.

DAD, IF YOU ARE LOOKING DOWN AT ME, I AM TRULY SORRY!

THE DAY DAD DIED

I remember well the day dad died

I was miles away, not by his side

The year: 2016; the day: the ninth of June

I tried to get there, but he left too soon

I thought of memorial day, just a week before,

I told him I didn't want to talk to him anymore.

We had an argument' about some stupid political thing

Those last words I spoke, in my heart, still sting

My plan was to somehow get to his bedside that day

Then, beg his forgiveness for the things I did say

I never got the chance to undo what I had done

He never heard the finale "I love you" from this son

With this guilt, I must live for the rest of my days

This guilt, which so heavy on my heart, does weigh

William Arthur Nahmens

MOTHER LEFT
About the Poem

I wrote "Mother Left" After watching my Mother passed away after weeks of fighting to hold on. She had a tumor in her intestines, and due to her age (93), they did not want to operate. She was put on hospice with strong pain medication and died at home surrounded by 6 of her 7 Children. She fought death all the way to the end, refusing to go. At one point, the hospice nurse said, "I don't understand how she is hanging on; she has enough medication in her to kill a rhino!" Mom just refused to go. It wasn't until we were all there at her side that she finally gave up the ghost. I remember standing there, feeling helpless as

"Mother Left"

MOTHER LEFT

Mother left today, although I begged her to stay

She noded slowly, closing her eyes as she went away

I cried out, "Mommy." Even though it sounded silly,

I pleaded, "Please stay! Don't leave your little Billy."

I squeezed her hand tightly, refusing to let her go

Fighting back the tears that were starting to flow

"Be strong for me," she once asked

This was proving to be too great a task

I had watched for weeks as in pain she suffered

Keeping her stoic demeanor, seeming unruffled

Once, she whispered in my ear, "I love you, you know."

"Just promise me when it is time, you will let me go."

I said I would but feared that promise could not last

Unsure I could do it, as my strength was failing fast

Feeling lost and helpless, I just stood and wept

As with one last sigh, mother left.

William Arthur Nahmen

LET ME GO
About the Poem

I wrote "Let Me Go" after watching my Mother pass away. She fought so hard to stay alive (I believe for the sake of her children). We didn't want her to go, so she tried so hard for our sakes. She was suffering so. Finally, when all her children were gathered around her (except one), and we all told her it was ok to go…She left. I don't want to suffer so. I just want everyone to tell me it is okay for me to go, assuring me that they will be alright.

LET ME GO

When it is my time for that final curtain to fall

Please let me go in peace, is what I ask; that is all

Don't try to keep me here out of your need or guilt

Be happy for our time together and the relationship we built.

Don't dwell on what loneliness or sorrows may lay ahead,

Remember our past, the happiness and joy we shared instead.

You know I love you, and if you ask me not to go, I will fight to stay,

For you, I would do that, but please don't ask; don't let me suffer that way.

I hope you understand my reasoning and are not offended,

I ask, please, don't keep me between life and death suspended.

I fought the good fight, fighting hard and standing as long as I could,

Not for myself but for your sake, I fought to stay longer than I should.

Realize now, at last, my fight is ended, the time has come for me to leave,

My last request is: Sit with me, tell me it's ok to go, then just let me go…please.

William Arthur Nahmens

A DAD HURTS TOO

About the Poem

This was written by an anonymous writer. I have read or heard it a number of different ways, but this version has always been my personal favorite. Oftentimes, we men are looked upon as non-feeling or cold. We are looked upon for strength when tragedy strikes. People don't see the struggle we go through to keep up a strong exterior for the sake of others. Don't be fooled by what you see or hear; Men do cry and feel pain. We are just told that we must be strong for our loved one's sake. We must keep it all in, for it is a sign of weakness to let our pain or tears show.

NOT TRUE! LET THE PAIN AND TEARS FLOW!

A DAD HURTS TOO

Dedicated to every Dad who ever felt the pain of loss

People don't always see the tears a Dad cries,

His heart is broken, too, when his beloved child dies.

He tries to hold it together and tries to be strong,

Even though his whole world has gone wrong,

He holds his wife as her tears fall,

Comforting her through it all,

He goes through his day doing what he is supposed to do,

But a piece of his heart has been ripped away, too,

So, when he's alone, he lets out his pain,

And his tears come down like pouring rain,

His world has crashed in all around him,

All that was once bright has gone completely dim,

He searches for answers, but none are to be found,

Who helps a Dad up when he hits the ground,

He just keeps smiling, hiding the tears,

As he struggles trying to hold in his fears,

But what you see on the outside is not always real,

Men don't always show how they really feel.

He must be strong for the sake of others,

But Dads hurt too, not just the Mothers

Anonymous

THE MOMENT THAT YOU DIED

About the Poem

I found this poem after my Mother passed away (my Sister Terri posted it on Facebook). The Author is unknown, but the words moved me so much that I wanted to include them here. You can't begin to understand how it feels to lose someone you love. Only someone who went through it themselves can ever understand how it feels. There is a big empty hole in your heart that just won't heal; learning to live with the pain is all you can hope for. This poem put my feelings into words better than I could have. I could feel the writer's pain through their choice of words.

THANK YOU, TERI, FOR FINDING THIS

THE MOMENT THAT YOU DIED

The moment that you died
My heart was torn into two
One side filled with heartache
The other died with you.

I often lie awake at night.
When the world is fast asleep, and
Take a walk down memory lane
With tears on my cheeks.

Remembering you is easy.
I do it every day.
But missing you is heartache.
That never goes away.

I hold you tightly within my heart
And there you will remain
Until the joyous day arrives
That we will meet again.

Anonymous

SECTION TWO

LOVE

YOU NEVER KNEW
About the Poem

I wrote this for a girl I practically grew up with. She always looked at me more like a brother. I always saw myself as her knight in shining armor. Many times, I defended her honor, yet I remained nothing more than a friend. She found her one true love and married him, while I, on the other hand, have given up on love. After two failed marriages and a ton of failed relationships, I know I will never find mine, for I already found her, and her heart will always belong to another. All I can do is be happy for her; she found true love, and she so deserves it. He has given her much more than I could ever have, and for that, I am eternally grateful.

YOU NEVER KNEW

You have known me almost your whole life through

Yet the love I hold in my heart, you never knew

I was always there; your honor to defend

But to you, I have never been more than a friend.

Your knight in shining armor, I so wanted to be

Still, only a friend was all you could ever see

You kissed me once so many long years ago

What meant nothing to you still sets my heart aglow

I remember the time I asked you to a dance

When you said yes, I thought I stood a chance

All my fond hopes so quickly did fade

to dance with you, I was just too afraid

That night, you wore a dress of velvet blue

When I hear "blue velvet," I still think of you.

There was a time I was going to ask for your hand,

Your mother stopped me; why, I never did understand

In a vain attempt to forget you, I married another

but my heart has always belonged to you and no other

On your wedding day, there were many tears cried

But the ones I shed, I had to keep buried deep inside

I see you from time to time, even still today

Those feelings of love have never faded away.

You always greet me with a big hug and a nice smile

Unknown to you, my heart is breaking all the while.

The love in my heart for you will always burn

But that love I know will never be returned

I have searched for just the right words to tell you,

I never found them, so you never knew.

William Arthur Nahmens

TO TRISH
About the Poem

I wrote "To Trish" for a special woman I thought I wanted to marry. I had broken it off and got back together with her so many times I lost count. While home on leave from the Marines, I asked her to marry me. She said "yes," but then she would not wear or take my engagement ring. The funny part was I didn't really buy it for her. I bought it from some scam guy while on Liberty. (he was selling them from the trunk of his car). He said, "I know a handsome guy like you has a girl back home." It was payday, so I bought it without any plans of getting engaged to Trish. In fact, if you read the poem in this section, "You Never Knew," you will see I tried to Marry someone else. Her Mother told me, "No, she is not for you". I went the next day and asked Trish (after all, we were going together) when she would not wear it; I turned to another woman whom my mother had just introduced me to. She said yes, our marriage lasted six years. I know Trish and I were not meant to be; I just feel bad about how I just "dumped" her with no explanation; I just never called her again. I tried to write a letter of apology (years later, during my 2nd marriage). It came back "return to sender, undeliverable." It had obviously been opened. I still have an aching need to apologize to Trish.

TO TRISH

Wherever she may be

You loved me once so very long ago

I was such a fool to ever let you go.

You said you couldn't wear my ring

I acted like it didn't mean a thing

out of my wounded, foolish pride

I heartlessly just cast you aside

I know now I didn't understand

I was immature not much of a man

If love is strong, all things it will endure

Mine was just too weak, so you felt unsure

I so regret the way I treated you

It was an awful, cruel thing to do

I left without telling you why

I left without even saying goodbye

many things I long to say to you

Not for the past to try and undo;

My reason is pure, it is just this:

I long to say, "I am so sorry, Trish."

William Arthur Nahmen

CHANGE OF SEASON
About the Poem

I wrote "Change of Season" after my second marriage ended. I remember watching the leaves as they went from hanging on trees with their bright, beautiful fall colors to laying on the ground, brown and dying, blown around by the wind. I recalled (as I watched this transformation) the failed marriages and the many failed relationships in my life. I realized that just as the leaves were dying, so too dying was the hope for true love in my life time.

CHANGE OF SEASON

Leaves once hanging brightly on trees.

Now, on the ground, lay dying.

Driven by the winds of change

They do their dance of death

Signaling the end of a season

So, too, my love

William Arthur Nahmens

A BIG EMPTY HOLE

About the Poem

I wrote "A Big Empty Hole" during a time when I was trying to describe the emptiness I felt in my heart and how I tried to fill it. As I was writing, the poem kept turning away from "trying to fill it" to how I felt the hole just grew more day by day, year by year, and that soon there would be nothing left of me except the empty hole.

A BIG EMPTY HOLE

A big empty hole where a loving heart used to be,

The world came along and cut it right out of me.

This very lonely heart searched for love but in vain,

Seeking out love yet finding nothing but sorrow and pain.

Love is a very cruel taskmaster, demanding your attention,

It takes from you all while denying you its sweet affection.

With the dawn of a new day, the quest begins anew,

To end my search now is something I just cannot do.

"other's have found true love," I keep telling myself,

So, I search ever harder, trying to keep true to myself.

With each passing day, the hope within dies a little more,

Waiting for the day, I just refuse to open another door.

Until, at last, the big empty hole where my heart used to be,

Overtakes me, body and soul, leaving nothing of what was once me.

William Arthur Nahmens

LOVE; ELUSIVE AND FLEETING
About the Poem

I wrote "Love; Elusive and Fleeting" during my "searching for love" phase (at the time that most of the poems in the section were written). It describes my fruitless attempt to find love. Love has always seemed to remain just outside of my grasp. Still, I keep reaching for it, trying to catch it as love always escapes me, leaving me "looking like a hopeless sap."

LOVE; ELUSIVE AND FLEETING

Love is such an elusive, fleeting thing

You pursue, believing happiness it will bring

As elusive as a butterfly you chase in a meadow

As hard to catch as any fleeting, fading shadow

Yet you search for it like some desired treasure

To find and possess it, you will take any measure

So, you press ever onward, striving to find that feeling

Sure, that once it is found, your heart will begin healing

You search the world for love, realizing your search is in vain

For all you ever find or feel is the pain of a love unobtained

You cry yourself to sleep, ending your day the way it began

With the dawning of the new day, the search begins again

Hoping to find it this time, yet believing you never will

Nonetheless, you are ever driven to search for it, still

Love, like the butterfly, stays just beyond your grasp

Leaving you cold and alone, feeling like a sap

William Arthur Nahmens

SO MANY LOVE
About the Poem

I wrote "So Many Loves" one day as I sat thinking back on all the girls/women who touched my life and how I thought I could not "live without them." Still, no matter how much I wished for love, it never came my way, or if it did, it never lasted. Now, I find myself looking back and wishing that just one of them could have been meant for me and happiness could have been mine.

SO MANY LOVES
Remembering past Loves

Remembering those I have loved in the past

From the very first and ending with the last.

I can honestly say I clearly remember them all

Although I know that some of them may not recall

My first crush was Alice, then Patty, with eyes of blue

I had it bad. I remember me; however, she quickly outgrew

Then there was Jennifer, Peggy, Kathy, and a Linda or two,

There was Robyn, Vickie, Ellen, Elaine, Carolyn, and even Sue

Along with Janice, Janet, Jane, Maggie, Bobbie, Becky, and Jill,

Most had no interest in me; I dated a few, yet each left me empty, still

There was Donna, Mickey, and Lisa, but the loveliest of all was Trish

Herr's is the memory that haunts me the most; for her, I so coldly
dismissed

There was Cindy, Pam Kelly, Lynn, and Lenora, and it ends with
Christine

married twice, first Cindy, then Christine. The pain of marriage was
unforeseen

So now here I sit alone and unloved, looking back at the many women
who touched my life

Remembering fondly each one in turn, wondering why not one could
ever be or stay my wife

William Arthur Nahmens

LOVE, A MYSTERY

About the Poem

I wrote "Love, A Mystery" after pondering how love is so fragile and yet
so strong at the same time. I originally titled the poem "Love, a Fragile
thing" but changed it after writing the last line. I realized that the poem
really wasn't just about love being fragile but, instead, was about love
being both fragile and strong at the same time. So, I changed the first
two lines and went with the mystery of love instead of love's weakness.

LOVE, A MYSTERY

Love is so strange and such a mystery

It has been talked about all through history

It is often called a fragile thing

Easily broken as a butterfly's wing

It is just as easy to crush as a rose petal

Yet love, if true, is stronger than any metal

But if it is not handled with tender care

It will fade away until it is no longer there

But a love that is pure can and will endure

It will overcome any obstacle; rest assured

Love flourishes where honesty abounds

Without honesty, love cannot be found

What makes love such a mystery to me?

So fragile yet so powerful, you see

William Arthur Nahmens

NEVER AGAIN
About the Poem

I wrote "Never Again" as a goodbye to love. I decided that never again would I seek Love. It is just too painful, and the cost is much too high. Some people will read this and tell me I am much too cynical about love. I do not think that I am a cynic no; I believe I am a realist.

NEVER AGAIN

Never again will I allow anyone to cause me such pain

Never again will I, by love's cold, cruel sword, be slain

My heart I take back, no longer yours to wound or destroy

At last, it has been emptied; of love, it is completely devoid

My heart is now dead to love, so move along if you please

You have accomplished your task of knocking me to my knees

My heart will never venture forward to look for love

It has crashed to the ground, much like a wounded dove

It lays still, broken and dying; any attempt to revive it is in vain

Laying cold and dead it shall remain, to seek love never again

William Arthur Nahmens

THE WALL
About the Poem

I wrote "The Wall," sort of as a sequel to "The Child Within". It is about the walls I have built up over the years to keep people out (a change from the "Child Within| as the walls in that poem were to keep me safe. I guess when it is all said and done, no matter how you phrase it, walls keep people from getting to close to me.

THE WALL

With pieces of my broken heart for bricks

Using my wasted tears to mix the motor with

Brick by brick, I stack one upon the other

Filling in cracks with the tearfilled motor mix

Stacking the bricks ever higher, I build the wall

I keep building until a way in no longer remains

Keeping me from both life and love's cruel ways

Life's arrows hit the wall, falling harmlessly to the ground

While love's cruel sword shatters as it strikes the mighty wall

No more will I feel the pain of a broken heart

Not another wasted tear shall fall from these eyes

For I am safely behind "the wall."

William Arthur Nahmens

LOVE SO DISTANT AND OBSCURE
About the Poem

I wrote "Love so Distant and Obscure" after giving up on ever finding love and happiness. The title (and the idea) came to me one day when I was listening to "All by Myself" by Eric Carmen. I identified with his opening line: "When I was young, I never needed anyone, and making love was just for fun. Those days are gone." I realized that those words described my life when I was young, but now that I am old, I no longer feel that way. Breaking hearts to me meant nothing back then. Today, I long and crave companionship. I would trade all those women from my past for just one who would want me and stay with me, ending my life of secluded loneliness. In the song "all by myself," the singer uses a line that says, "Love so distant and obscure, remains the cure." I feel the same way.

LOVE SO DISTANT AND OBSCURE

All my life, I have pursued love that has remained distant and obscure

Ever reaching for it with arms outstretched yet ever failing all the more

Time and time again, chasing it like a butterfly you never can quite catch

With my heart ever aching and full of pain, I remain in my state, unattached

Yet I can never give up, reaching for it no matter how unobtainable

Each failed attempt haunts me, staying in my heart, so unforgettable

With each passing year, elusive love slips ever further away

Yet I remain, ever stubborn, hoping that "this could be my day."

Unable to just give up, forced to chase this fleeting thing called love

I keep running, chasing after it, trying to catch the ever-fleeting dove

Despite all my efforts, love still remains so distant and obscure

The chase leaves me broken and unsure. How much more can I endure?

William Arthur Nahmens

LAST
About the Poem

"Last" was written for the reason, just as it reads, to mark the last time
I would allow anyone to hurt or break my heart again. It was written,
again, at the low part of my life when I felt like love was just another
weapon used on someone's unsuspecting heart. So I decided SHE
would be the last to destroy my heart and life.

LAST

Looking back over the years at Love's painful past

I have decided that this time will be the very last

Love, ever fleeting, was never meant for me

Time and time again, it has escaped me, you see

Filled with love and hope, I willingly gave my heart

To have it handed back to me destroyed and torn apart

So, I have decided: Alone, I will remain and always be

I have closed my heart, placing it under lock and key

There it shall remain, waiting for eternity to come to an end

I will no longer dream of love or allow it my heart to offend

I will never again feel love's painful sting as in years past

I will never fall for another empty promise; this time was the last

William Arthur Nahmens

SECTION THREE

LIFE

"A YOUNG MAN ASKS HIS GRANDFATHER"
About the Story

I found this on the internet. I do not know who wrote it. I have been asked this question by my Nephews, Nieces, and other young people. I found this response to be the best one I have ever heard. I included it here to give the younger generations something to think about.

"A YOUNG MAN ASKS HIS GRANDFATHER"

A young man asked his grandfather, "Grandpa, how did you live in the past without technology...
without computers,
without an Internet connection,
without Big Screen TVs,
without air conditioners,
no cell phones?"
Grandpa answered:
"While your generation lives today...
there are no prayers,
there is no compassion,
there is no respect,
no real education,
there is no personality,
there is no shame at all,
there is no modesty,
there is no honesty.
We, the people born between the years 1940-1980, were the blessed ones.
Our lives are a living proof."
* While playing and riding a bike, we have never worn a helmet.
* Before school, then, we played and again after school until dusk and hardly ever watched television.
* We played with real friends, not virtual friends.
* If we were thirsty, we would drink tap water or water from the hose, not mineral water.
* We never worried even as we shared the same cup of juice with four friends.
* We never gained weight by eating plates of pasta every day.
* Nothing happened to our feet despite roaming barefoot.
* We never used food supplements to stay healthy.
* We used to make our own toys and play with them.
* Our parents were not rich. They gave love, not stuff.
* We never had a cell phone, DVD, game console, Xbox, video game, PC, internet, chat . . . but we had true friends.
* We visited our friends without being invited and shared and enjoyed the food with them.
Parents lived nearby to take advantage of family time.
* We may have had black-and-white photos, but you can find colorful memories in these photos.

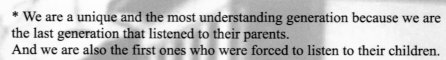

* We are a unique and the most understanding generation because we are the last generation that listened to their parents.
And we are also the first ones who were forced to listen to their children.
* We are a limited edition!
Take advantage of us. Learn from us. We are a treasure destined to disappear soon.

DESIDERATA
About the Poem

This poem "Desiderata" was rumored to be found in a church in the 1600s but was actually written in 1927 by Max Ehrmann, a poet and lawyer from Terre Haute, Indiana. The word desiderata is Latin for "things that are desired." Ehrmann said he wrote it for himself "because it counsels those virtues I felt most in need of." It was set to music in i1971 (by Les Crane with music by composer Fred Werner and concept and lyrics by David C. Wilson). It is a spoken-word song with sung refrains and instrumental accompaniment. I included it in this book not to lay claim to it but rather because it became a driving force in my life during those difficult teenage years. I hope it inspires readers of this book as it has inspired me.

DESIDERATA

Go placidly amid the noise and haste,
And remember what peace there may be in silence.
As far as possible without surrender,
Be on good terms with all persons.
Speak your truth quietly and clearly, and listen to others -
Even the dull and ignorant, they, too, have their story.
Avoid loud and aggressive persons - they are vexations to the spirit.
If you compare yourself with others, you may become vain and bitter,
For always there will be greater and lesser persons than yourself.
Enjoy your achievements as well as your plans.
Keep interested in your own career -
However humble, it is a real possession in the changing fortunes of time.
Exercise caution in your business affairs,
For the world is full of trickery.
But let this not blind you to what virtue there is.
Many people strive for high ideals,
and everywhere, life is full of heroism.
Be yourself.
Especially do not feign affection neither be cynical about love.
For in the face of all aridity and disenchantment,
It is as perennial as the grass.
Take kindly the council of the years,
Gracefully surrendering the things of youth.
Nurture strength of spirit to shield you in sudden misfortune,
But do not distress yourself with imaginings -
Many fears are borne of fatigue and loneliness.
Beyond a wholesome discipline, be gentle with yourself.
You are a child of the universe.
No less than the trees and the stars, you have a right to be here.
And whether or not it is clear to you,
No doubt the universe is unfolding as it should.
Therefore, be at peace with God, whatever you conceive him to be.
And whatever your labors and aspirations,
in the noisy confusion of life,
Keep peace with your soul.
With all its sham, drudgery, and broken dreams,
it is still a beautiful world.
Be careful. Strive to be happy.

Max Ehrmann

"A LITTLE POEM FOR SENIORS"

About the Poem

I found this little gem on the net. I do not know who wrote it, but it rang so true to me that I just had to add it here. It is in the humor section because it is both true and funny at the same time. I hope you enjoy it as much as I did.

A LITTLE POEM FOR SENIORS

So true it hurts

Another year has passed, and we are all a little older.

Last summer felt hotter; This winter feels much colder.

There was a time, not long ago, when life was quite a blast.

Now I fully understand about living in the past

We used to go to weddings, football games and lunches.

Now, we go to funeral homes and after-funeral brunches.

We used to go out dinning. And couldn't get our fill.

Now we ask for doggie bags, go home, and take a pill.

We used to often travel to places near and far.

Now we get sore asses from riding in the car.

We used to go to nightclubs and drink a little booze

Now we just stay home at night and watch the evening news.

That, my friend, is how life is, and now my tale is told.

Enjoy each day and live it up before you're just too damn old!

Unknown

"THIS AND THAT"
About the Poem

I wrote this Poem after a heated argument with someone very close to me. As the argument ensued and grew hotter and more intense, I realized that neither one of use really heard what the other one was saying. We both were hearing something else while, at the same time, the other one was speaking, preparing our response to what we thought we were hearing.

THIS AND THAT

Most arguments are because I said this, but you heard that,

We never listen to what the other is saying; what a sad epithet.

Instead, our mind is thinking of the response we plan to say,

Our thoughts and minds, from the conversation, start to stray.

Then misunderstanding enters the fray, bringing with it disdain,

Ending, where neither of us, from this silly argument, can refrain

Then, the simple misunderstanding evolves into a full-blown war.

Where there is no winner, unable to hear the other anymore.

We swear the other is to blame as we engage in heated combat,

All because I thought you said this, but you really said that.

William Arthur Nahmens

WHY DO I WASTE MY TIME?
About the Poem

I wrote "Why do I waste my Time" after thinking about why I write poetry. It is difficult to write, and I also struggle with both meaningful words and rhyming. I finally answered my question after reading what my poems are about.

WHY DO I WASTE MY TIME?

Why do I try to write poetry? Why do I sit and waste my time?

Struggling to find the right words, straining to make them rhyme.

Do I write for myself? From the depths of a broken heart?

Or is it for others? Trying to ease their pain in some small part.

Do I write because I think I have something clever to say?

Or do I write because to express myself, I have no other way?

Do I write from some very dark corner of a wounded Soul?

Or am I trying to let go of some forgotten pain? Is that my Goal?

Am I trying to tell others, "It is alright to sit and have a good cry"?

Or is it my attempt to show them it is not good to hold pain inside?

I write for the ones who have lost their way and find they have no choice,

I write for the ones that life has stolen their joy, and now they have no voice.

I write for the ones who have lost at love, and their dreams have been shattered.

I write for those whose pieces of their broken heart have been cruelly scattered.

So, I guess it is for all these reasons and more that I sit and waste my time.

Struggling to find the right words then straining to make them rhyme.

William Arthur Nahmens

LIFE SUCKS
About the Poem

I wrote "Life Sucks" after hearing it for years and starting to believe myself. Then, one day (as I sat feeling sorry for myself because of having cancer for the 3rd time), I REMEMBERED WHAT MY Mother had tried to teach me all my life. Life is what YOU make it. No one can make your life hard or easy unless you give them that power. Your life is yours. I still have cancer, and I still have good days and bad days, but I choose how I react to those 'bad days", choosing to, instead, live in the memory of the Good Days.

LIFE SUCKS

The phrase "life sucks, and then you die."

I heard it said but often wondered why

Who first said this: was it really meant?

Was it said after a rough life as someone went?

Was it merely said as tongue-in-cheek humor?

Was it said out of anger, or is it just a rumor?

I find life is what you make of it; if it sucks, that's on you

If your life is a waste and filled with pain. That is your choice, too

Life is life; it is neither hard nor easy, each has their own battle to fight

What looks easy to you may be hell for another. Am I wrong, or am I right

Each and every one of us has a life to live; if it's rough or sucks, look within

Don't spend your life in misery, blaming luck or fate for the state you're in

Life is what you make it; live for yourself and not for some other

Finally learning this now, after first hearing it from my own mother

William Arthur Nahmens

THE CHILD WITHIN
About the Poem

I wrote "The Child Within" in response to people asking me why I seem to have so many walls or barriers between me and the world. They would ask if the purpose of the walls was to keep them and the rest of the world out. Did I really want to cut myself off from everything? I tried to explain that the purpose of the walls was not to keep others out but rather to keep the child inside me safe. We all have an inner child that has been and still can be wounded, so we try our best to keep that part of us safe from harm. This was actually my first attempt at writing poetry.

THE CHILD WITHIN

Rising high against the horizon, they appear

Walls, standing tall, looking strong and mighty,

Seeing them, you say, "A mighty Knight must dwell within,"

You approach the walls and see they are made of hard granite,

Dark and cold to the touch, they are foreboding and unwelcoming,

As you touch them, you say, "A cold-hearted man must dwell within,"

Upon examining the walls, you find cracks, opening in the walls,

These walls, that were built in haste, offer little to no protection at all,

Seeing the flaws, you say, "Surely a careless man dwells within."

You enter, unsure what you will find: Knight, Cold or careless man,

Finding none of these, you find, instead, a child laying at the very
center

Listening for sound, looking for movement, he lies trembling and
afraid,

He wonders, "Will my walls hold? Or will I feel the painful sting of life
again?"

William Arthur Nahmens

LOOKING BACK
About the Poem

One day, I was considering all the battles and struggles I faced in my life, it resulted in the writing of this poem. I realized that reliving them or trying to fight them over again changed nothing, for it is impossible to undo what has been done. Yesterday is only a memory, and tomorrow is but a dream; all we have is today. Live for today and leave yesterday where it belongs. IN THE PAST!

LOOKING BACK

Looking back over the years

I have some regrets but no tears

there are things I could have done better

I didn't always follow the rules to the letter

It matters not what others may say or think

No one knows the bitter waters I had to drink

Many battles I had to fight; some I lost, some I won

But I fought each one to the end; what's done is done

I will not go back to try to fight or relive them again

That would be a waste, and for what reason? To what end?

To recall the sting of a defeat or the joy of a victory;

Changes nothing today and will just bring me misery.

So, don't dwell on what was; leave the past in the past

Work on today's problems, for today is tomorrow's past

William Arthur Nahmens

THAT'S JUST THE WAY IT GOES
About the Poem

I wrote this one after thinking back on all the battles I have won or lost in life and love. I thought about how sometimes I had the snot knocked out of me, sometimes I knocked the snot out of someone else, sometimes I got the worst end in a relationship and how love left me broken and bruised, while other times I was the one doing the breaking as bruising as I left some one behind. It really put it all in perspective for me. Sometimes each one of us wins, and sometimes we don't. It is a universal law, and "That's just the way it goes."

THAT'S JUST THE WAY IT GOES

Sometimes you win, sometimes you lose, you never know what life throws.

All you can do is take the punch and just hold on, for that's just the way it goes.

When life hits you hard and knocks you to your knees, if it hurts, don't let it show.

Just pick yourself up, brush yourself off, smile and say, "That's just the way life goes."

When you win a battle, don't gloat or boast; just take the win as your own

Walk away from the fight. Knowing you won and say, "That's just the way it goes."

When you lose at love and, your heart is crushed, much like the petals of a rose

Wipe the tear from your eye, smile, and say, "Sometimes, that's just the way it goes."

For the next time around, you may be the one breaking someone's heart; who knows?

This time, it was you; next time, it will be them, for that's just the way love goes.

Remember this: Life is not always peaches and cream, nor is it all heartaches and woes.

Whatever life hands you, just tell yourself, "Sometimes, that's just the way life goes."

William Arthur Nahmens

THE OLD MAN IN THE MIRROR
About the Poem

"The Old Man in the Mirror" is about how (in my mind, heart, and soul) I still felt like a young twenty-year-old ready to take on the world, but the reflection I see in the mirror is an old man telling me it is time to slow down. My body echoes this sentiment by reminding me of the many injuries I had sustained over the years. Combined with the fact my eyesight is going, my hearing is going, my strength is fading, and my legs are growing weaker by the day. I look at that "Old Man" in the mirror and tell him, "Not yet, old timer" I am not ready to lay down and give up." So I step outside, ready to face the day, feeling young and full of life; the next morning, it starts all over again!

THE OLD MAN IN THE MIRROR

Every morning, as I stand and look in the mirror, I wonder who it is I
see?

Where am I? Why, myself, do I not see? Who is this old man looking
back at me?

In my mind, body, heart, and soul, I am still a young man just twenty
years old.

While the old man in the mirror tells me my youth I have squandered
and sold

The body chimes in with a tinge of pain, recalling every bone I broke
over the years.

Then the brain screams out! "Accept it, you're an old man," as my eyes
fill with tears.

The legs, though they are trying, are weak; they struggle to hold up the
old man.

Arms and hands, once powerful and strong, are weak but willing to do
what they can.

Eyes that are now dim and foggy recall another time when they were
clear and bright.

Ears that once could hear a pin drop now join in the argument to just
give up the fight.

Just as hope is fading, that twenty-year-old spirit rises up, giving this
old body a new spark.

Suddenly, the old man from the mirror fades as another new day
begins, another new start.

William Arthur Nahmens

MY MUSKEGO
About the poem

I wrote this poem after my 50th Class reunion for Muskego High Class of 1973. As I traveled through my "old neighborhood," I barely recognized it. The public park (Park No.1) where I once swam, fished, and went sledding was now a private park. Most of the old land marks were gone. I tried donating two of the books I had written (one of which is an autobiography of how I overcame losing my vision) were rejected by the school I graduated from. The City has grown so large that it has lost its innocence and small-town appeal. I felt so out of place in the city in which I had grown up. My heart and soul cry for "My Muskego."

MY MUSKEGO

Even though I moved away from you so many years ago,
You have always held a special place in my heart and soul.
As a young boy, your many fields, woods, and streets I did roam;
No matter how far I went from the house, I always felt I was home.
The terror I inflicted on neighbors through those rebellious teenage
years
I spent many a day in regret, wishing I could undo them, with falling
tears
Every time I return, my heart both longs and breaks for my Muskego
The fields and woods I once roamed break my heart, for they are gone
The park where I once played and swam is now a private park; I'm not
allowed in
The Muskego I roamed as a boy is gone; I can't tell where the old ends
and the new begins
When I return to see my Muskego, I no longer feel I am at home; this I
don't understand
Every time I go back to "My Muskego," it hurts, for I feel like a stranger
in some foreign land!

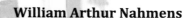

William Arthur Nahmens

THE PRIVATE WAR

About the Poem

I was inspired to write this poem by two things. One was a poster I saw on a wall that read, "Be kinder than Necessary. Everyone is fighting some kind of battle (or something along those lines). The other was a picture of dog tags that read, "I hope you win the war you are fighting. The one you never tell anyone about, the one you fight in silence." I thought about how each and every one of us is fighting some type of personal battle that we rarely (if ever) talk about.

THE PRIVATE WAR

Each and every one of us has or is fighting our own private war

We battle through each day, fighting hard our spirits to restore

At night, bitter tears we shed alone in the dark so others won't see

In the morning, we put on painted smiles; that is the way it must be

What is it that haunts you? What battle are you fighting deep within?

Have you given up? Telling yourself, "This is a battle I just can't win?"

It may be the battle of addiction; each time you say, "This will be the last."

With each and every failure, you lose hope of ever escaping from your past.

Or could it be the loss of a loved one or maybe even the death of a child?

you try to battle through while feeling that part of you is dead, all the while

Are you that Veteran who battles PTSD? Trapped, fighting an endless war?

Fighting hard every day until finally, you scream, "I just can't take no more!"

Whatever the secret war you're fighting, the one you never tell anyone about

Don't ever stop fighting until the war is won and sweet victory you can shout!

William Arthur Nahmens

BUT WHY THE MARINES?
About the Poem

This poem came about in an attempt to answer the question I have so often been asked. "Why did you join the Marines?" People who knew me in my younger years often saw me as weak, quiet, and not fitting in. Silently, I took their abuse without fighting back or standing up for myself. This caused a deep-seated hatred to form and relationships to fail. I finally had to prove to the world, but more importantly, myself, that I was not what everyone saw on the outside. I also needed to rid myself of this hidden anger. When I was made Sergeant, I knew I had proved I was a leader of men, not a follower. I proved I had what it took to be a Marine. Not everyone tries to make it through Boot Camp. Not just anyone can earn the right to the title "Marine." It is a rite of passage that takes a special breed to see it through to the end.

BUT WHY THE MARINES?

This question I oft time have been asked

I struggle with the answer, for it is not exact

Growing up, lost in a world of misguided and misdirected anger

At war with the world, the hatred in me spreading like a cancer

Many years of abuse and bullying left me angry and ashamed

I wasted many years in anger, thinking everyone else was to blame

Afraid someone might see, I hid this hate deep within my hardened
soul

I found myself fighting a daily battle, just trying to keep it all under
control

All those many years of abuse at home, as well as from others

Took a heavy toll, hatred, as it builds, a soft heart it will smother

With my sulence mistaken for weakness and a heart as hard as a rock

I lived in this lonely world I built, choosing to live alone in the dark

Then suddenly, one day, out of nowhere, a light did brightly appear

I needed to show the world I had overcome and conquered my fears

I felt I had to prove to others there was more to me than what they'd
seen

More importantly, I needed to prove to myself I had what it took to be
a Marine

So, in answer to the question:

THAT'S WHY THE MARINES!

William Arthur Nahmens

THE MARINE WITHIN
About the Poem

I wrote this poem after talking to aging Marine Veterans and realizing that they still felt they could "kick ass and take names!" That what others see on the outside in no way reflects what we feel on the inside. As I age, I feel this same fire burning within me. "I can still whip the world," I tell myself. And make statements to that effect every day. The body may be getting older, but the Marine living inside has not aged a day since first earing the title "Marine".

THE MARINE WITHIN

Take a close look at me; what do you see?

A broken-down old man? Or do you see a marine?

Within this aged body that you labeled useless and decayed,

Beats the heart of a virile, young warrior, standing unafraid

Deep in his soul, the lust for battle burns red-hot

His only purpose in life is to fight, for that is his lot.

His entire life has been spent preparing for war

Searching for some lost cause that he will die for

His strength has not waned, nor has his eye dim

He stands ready for any challenge thrown at him

His body he has given to be broken and bruised

His mind is prepared to do whatever he must do

So, while on the outside quite useless, I may seem

Look closer for deep inside beats the heart of a marine!

SEMPER FI!

William Arthur Nahmens

WHEN YOUR COUNTRY CALLED

About the Poem

The Original title of this poem, which also appears in this book, was written for a very special "Brother in-arms." I rewrote it after remember my my fisrt visit to "The Wall". It was heartbreaking as I watched men looking for a name on that wall, then touching the name as they wept over a fallen friend. I watched women crying over lost husbands, Fathers, and Mothers crying over lost Children. If you have never been to "The Wall" in Washington, DC, you need to go. The traveling wall does not do the real thing justice. It is both awe-inspiring and heartbreaking as you realize each name on the wall is someone's Son, Daughter, Husband, Wife, or close friend who didn't make it back home.

WHEN YOUR COUNTRY CALLED

That day, when your country called,

You were there to answer that call

Not sure of what the future did hold

For others, you willingly risked your soul.

Leaving your life for some faraway land

For others, risking your life upon foreign sand!

Each and every day, with every single breath

You stood in the gap, facing certain death.

Your blood spilled upon foreign ground

Still, you got up; you wouldn't stay down.

When you left, you left part of your soul

No one can ever know how heavy the toll

Your eyes have seen things others have not

Your soul has bled in ways others will not.

You are not just another name on "the wall."

But one of the sacred fallen who gave it their all.

William Arthur Nahmens

GONE AND THEN FORGOTTEN
About the Poem

This poem was written after searching for a monument that once stood in a city. It commemorated the Janesville Tank Battalion (from Janesville, Wisconsin). These 99 men were sent to the Philippines during World War II. My great-uncle was part of that group. Some died during the Bataan Death March. Some died in a POW Camp (My Uncle was among those). Only 35 of the 99 returned home alive. I was trying to research a book I was planning on writing about my Great Uncle and the rest of the 99. When I went to Janesville to take pictures of the two monuments (one was in front of the old National Guard Amory, and the other was downtown), I could not locate them. I later learned the one in front of the Amory was removed by the new owners. The one downtown was blocked off by construction (but at least it was still standing). I went to the Veterans Park to see if anything was there. There is no monument for WWI, WWII, or the Korean War. The only 2 monuments located there were for Vietnam and the war on terrorism. I thought it was sad how we are forgetting our men and women who served in long past wars. I made a pledge to NEVER forget them as long as I am alive.

GONE AND THEN FORGOTTEN

TO THE HEROES OF WARS PAST

Whenever the wars of this Nation have beckoned, there has been someone to answer.

Ready to leave their homes and their families to go and fight a war they didn't ask for

Some of them were lost, never returning home, while those that did would never be the same.

They fought our battles, sacrificing to keep us safe; to forget them now is just a shame.

Yet day after day, year after year, name after name, fades from memories, falling into a void.

As day after day, year after year, another monument is taken down or simply just destroyed.

Who will remember those brave Americans after their generation is gone?

Who will remember their sacrifice, tell their stories, or sing their praises in song?

If we forget our heroes or forget where we came from by forgetting our past.

Be assured we will be condemned to repeat history, and that will be our downfall at last.

As long as I am alive, I will never allow them to slip into the dark abyss of death.

I will keep them alive until the last drop of blood leaves my veins, until my last breath.

William Arthur Nahmens

DEATH BEFORE DISHONOR
About the Poem

I wrote this poem as an attempt to give others a peak into the mindset of a Marine.

The phrase comes code that the Samurai of ancient Japan lived by. They would rather die than bring dishonor to themselves, their family, or to the Samurai. Marines have this same mindset. We would die than to bring dishonor to God, our Country, or our beloved Corps.

DEATH BEFORE DISHONOR

Death before Dishonor is not just something Marines say,

It is the code each one of us lives by every single day

We are prepared to die for God, Country, and Corps

We don't just give 100 percent; we give much more

Choosing to fight to the death rather than live in Dishonor,

To try to convince us to give in and quit, Don't even bother.

For each Marine has in his heart, "Never surrender of my own free will."

This is the force that drives every Marine, for it has been deeply instilled.

For their beloved Corps, every Marine will fight and die

Living and dying for honor, much like the Ancient Samurai.

When you hear a Marine say, "Death before Dishonor," remember this

A Marine will fight to the bitter end because he doesn't know how to quit.

William Arthur Nahmens

WAR, IS A BEAST

About the Poem

I wrote "War is a Beast" after watching the war in Ukraine after Russia invaded. I watched the death and destruction of the innocent as well as the men and women spilling their blood, and for what? Because someone wanted something more than what they had. I looked back through history; it seemed to me that this theme was present in every war ever fought. Some groups of people wanted something from another group of people and were willing to use force to get it. I pray that someday we can finally live together in peace and harmony with each other. I know this is impossible. However, for as long as hate and greed live in the heart of man, peace is impossible.

WAR, IS A BEAST

War is a beast, an indiscriminate killer. it cares not who dies

It cares not who it leaves cold and alone, who mourns or cries

Father, mother, sister, brother, husband, wife, son or daughter

War does not care which have died or how many are slaughtered

War feeds on heartache and pain. It is, after all, an uncaring beast

Feeding upon the pain and grief of others. Death, to it, is a grand feast

Using the blood of the fallen and the tears of the innocent for drink

The beast that is war is much crueller than you would ever think

The beast calls us to battle, telling us it is a worthy cause we fight for

But every war ever fought arose from greed or someone wanting
more.

Til we learn to be content with what we have and put hatred in the
grave,

`the beast, will remain drunk on the tears of the innocent and the
blood of the brave

William Arthur Nahmens

FOR US, IT WAS...FOR THEM, IT WAS

About the Poem

I found this on the internet. While the Author is unknown, it really puts into perspective the difference between fighting a war and watching a war on Television. What combat Veterans have seen and gone through cannot be unseen or forgotten. Those who watched the war on Television can forget what they have seen; they have no idea the hell those who actually fought went through. They will never know or understand!

"FOR US, IT WAS...FOR THEM, IT WAS"

1964-1975

For us, it was the six o'clock news,

For them, it was a reality.

We called for a pizza,

They called for medics.

We watched children play,

They watched children die.

We learned of life,

They learned of death.

We served dinner,

They served their country.

Our passion was success,

Theirs was survival

We forgot,

They can't.

Anonymous

SECTION FOUR

FOR FAMILY AND FRIENDS

SOMEDAY
About the Poem

I do not know who wrote this, but it brought my Grandfather, mother and my Aunt Nancy to my mind. I remember watching my Grandfather and then my mom as they grew old. they would forget our names and often repeat the same story over and over again (and each time was slightly different than the last). My mom got to the point where she could not walk on her own anymore. Before she died, she whispered in my ear, "Be strong for me." I did the best I could, but this tough Marine was breaking down as she hung on. She did pass peacefully, but it still hurts...I miss her every day. My hope is that my own children will be there to help me through my final years and know how much I loved each one of them. My Mom's sister, (Nancy) suffered from lock jaw when she was a little girl. She, too, as she grows older, repeats the same stories over and over again. She tells us about her dreams (each one seems to be about her and John Wayne getting married). She broke her hip and is having difficulty walking. Her hearing and eyesight are all but gone. I need to re-read this every day to remind myself to help her and keep patient with her...It is not her choice to go through this. The least I can do is "walk with her" on this journey she is now forced to take.

SOMEDAY

Someday, I will be old. When that time comes,

Please be patient with me.

If I repeat a story hundreds of times, please don't

interrupt me; just listen.

After all, I used to tell You the same bedtime

Stories hundreds of times when you were little.

If I don't understand the latest Technology, don't make fun of me,

for I taught you how to eat, how to talk, how to walk, and, hopefully,

how to live a good life.

If I forget something or lose my place in a conversation,

give me time to remember. If I don't remember, that's ok too. All that matters Is that we're spending time together.

If my legs are too frail to carry me, help me walk. The same way

I helped you with your first steps.

And when my time comes to leave you, do not be sad.

Help me face my journey with love and patience.

I will thank you with a smile, a sign of my unending love.

Most importantly, never forget.

I LOVE YOU!

Unknown

THE STRANGER
About the Poem

I wrote "The Stranger" as a tribute to my Dad. I watched this once "mighty giant" grow weaker with each passing year. I remember how this man (who stood well over 6-foot-tall) was shrinking; his mighty frame was looking frail and weak. His voice could barely be heard.

Dad, I never realized how wise you were until you went away; I miss you every single day!

One last thought. My Super Hero could not fly, did not possess superhuman strength, nor did he have X-ray vision (although, at times, I thought he could see through the wall). He did not wear a cape, nor did his name contain the word "mam" (like Superman, Spiderman, or Batman).

I simply called him "Dad."

THE STRANGER

To my Father, who will always be larger than life in my eyes

I would sit for hours, just watching him as he worked

He was a giant of a man, standing ten feet tall, maybe taller

With two huge, powerful hands attached to arms like tree trunks

Using just one, he could lift a ton! Yet he used two when lifting me with
care

His voice was as loud as thunder! When he spoke, the whole world
shook!

****

I saw this once mighty giant just today; somehow, I seemed taller than
he

My hands looked bigger and stronger than His; he was unable to feed
himself

His once thunderous voice was but a whisper and could barely be
heard

As I looked upon this stranger lying in his bed, I was tempted to ask

"What have you done with my Dad?"

William Arthur Nahmens

A MOTHER'S HIDDEN TEAR
About the poem

I wrote "A Mother's Hidden Tear." After realizing the many tears, I caused my Mother to cry without ever seeing them. I only came to this realization many years after becoming an adult and feeling the pain of the hidden tears that I shed over the years over my own children. There is no one who can break your heart like a child can, and there is no child that can break your heart more than your own child can and will, someday at some time during your life together. Yet you will forgive that child. Why? Because they will ALWAYS be your child, come what may.

A MOTHER'S HIDDEN TEAR

To my Mother, for every hidden tear you have ever shed

How many times did I scream, "I hate you! I wish you were dead!"

Words of a child not spoken from the heart, not meaning what was said

With a Mother's smile, you'd say: "I hope you don't mean that dear."

Without another thought, I'd run off, never seeing the hidden tear

Through a childhood filled with illnesses, broken bones, and a cracked head

I came through manyrough times, some which could have left me dead

You were always there, with a reassuring smile, telling me not to fear

All the while, for my sake, never allowing me to see your hidden tear

Then, as suddenly as a storm arises, a rebellious teenager came along

Angry at the world, dead sure his parents knew nothing and were just wrong

You were there all through the hell of those teenage years

During which, you would shed many more hidden tears

One day, this teen grew, and a Marine was born

He left home, never giving a thought to the life he had torn

Coming home just to leave again over the years

Still somehow missing the hidden tears

Now I am grown with children of my own

They have all gone, leaving me alone.

Seeing them less and less with each passing year

leaves me to know the pain of the hidden tear

You raised me to be the man that I am

To always try hard and do the best I can

So, the best I can do for the rest of your years

tell you "I love you" and wipe away all of those hidden tears

William Arthur Nahmens

JENNIFER DAWN

About the Poem

I wrote this for my Daughter. I had lost touch with her over the years, and when I entered back into her life, I wasn't sure if she would want me in it after so many years. I wrote it to sound almost like a lost love. A father/Daughter relationship is on of the greatest mysteries in the world. The love a father has for his daughter is different than the love he feels for his son. He loves them both very deeply, but she will ALWAYS be his little girl, while eventually, he will come to look upon his son not as a little boy but as his equal as a man.

JENNIFER DAWN

Her Name is Jennifer Dawn,

I have loved her her whole life long.

I loved her from the start, falling at first glance.

My heart was so full of joy, it started to dance!

Suddenly, fear arose, and it took hold fast!

I wasn't sure, as a man, if I were up to the task.

I wanted so much for her, yet I was sure I would fail.

My courage was fading fast as I started turning pale.

As the days turned to years, I felt us bonding together.

I knew our hearts were one; come whatever.

We drifted apart; I lost her for a while.

But my heart could never forget that smile.

We found each other after many years, and I admit,

I was nervous. "Would she still love me, or did she forget?"

My fears quickly faded when she said, "I love you, Dad."

My heart again leapt with joy; I was relieved and glad!

Now that I have found my Jennifer Dawn again,

I will not lose her this time; I will hold on till the end!

William Arthur Nahmens

MY SON
About the Poem

I wrote this to my son, William Arthur Nahmens II. I realize I have failed him as a Father over the years. This poem is just a Dad's attempt to try and tell his son how he really feels about him. I hope he can someday find it in his heart to forgive me of my failings and know that I have *ALWAYS* loved him and *ALWAYS* will, come what may

MY SON

We share a name, and some might say there is not much else we have
in common,

We are more alike than different, and I hope you know you were never
forgotten.

The day I remember so well, April Twenty-four, Nineteen Hundred and
Seventy-Nine,

You were so tiny and small I was afraid to hold you, thinking I might
break your spine.

I cherish the sacred memories of times we spent together during your
early years,

When you left with your Mother, I cried so much I lost track of the
number of tears.

When you came back to me, I wanted to make it work. I thought I could
be a friend.

But being a Dad was harder than I thought, and that's what I needed to
be in the end.

You left again to go back with your Mother, taking with you what was
left of my heart,

Over the years, we fell out of touch; when I found you again, I didn't
know where to start.

We have reconnected again, and though we are miles apart,

Just remember you are never far away, for you are always in my heart.

Son, I know I have never told you how proud I am of you,

But I am! I have always loved you and am very proud of all you do.

I LOVE YOU, SON!

William Arthur Nahmens

MY BABY GIRL WAS MARRIED TODAY

About the Poem

I wrote "My Baby Girl was Married today" for My Daughter's (Sarah Gene) wedding day. I could not find a card that captured all I was feeling, so I wrote this instead. It really caught my feelings of watching her grow into womanhood and knowing she was no longer "My Baby Girl" but still realizing that my role as a father was still intact. I was not replaced. My job just changed a little.

MY BABY GIRL WAS MARRIED TODAY

With a soft whisper, I gave my daughter to be wed today

I always knew this day would come when I could not say

As I watched her through eyes filled with tears,

my mind wandered back over the years.

The first time I held her, so fragile and small;

my charge: "to love and protect her," seemed like an order much too tall.

Her first words I hold ever so dear;

The first time she said "Daddy" still echoes sweetly in my ear

Through fist steps, bike rides, and heartaches;

I could not always catch her; still, with each fall how my heart did break.

As the years went past, I felt no longer required;

I thought, as a father, I had been retired.

my feelings could not have been more wrong;

for the role of a father is lifelong.

Today, she stopped being my baby girl and became a Bride

It was time for me to give up my baby girl no matter how I cried

So, I gave up my charge and passed it to him as his wife;

"Love and protect her for the rest of her life."

William Arthur Nahmens

FOR CONNER

About the Poem

I wrote "For Conner" to my Grandson. I missed most of his life, but I did get to see him a few times through the years. I never really got to know him as much as I would have liked too. Still, I do know he is a gentle giant. I hope he will remember that his Grandpa always loved him and that I will always be there when he needs me. Even if I am gone from the face of this earth, I will find my way to him. Never forget; I do love you, Conner!

FOR CONNER

I was never there, missing the chance to watch you grow,

That doesn't mean I didn't love you; you should know.

I see in you a peaceful person with a gentle, kind spirit,

Just remember to live life to the fullest and never fear it.

If you ever feel that life is too hard and you want to quit,

Keep standing strong, fighting hard, and don't ever submit.

Whatever life may throw, never allow yourself to surrender,

Battle through to the end; don't let your life be torn asunder.

Above everything else, remember this: I will always be there,

You may not see me, but still, there I will be, so never despair.

I LOVE YOU, CONNER!

Always, Grandpa

William Arthur Nahmens

AUTUMN
About the Poem

This poem is dedicated to my Granddaughter Autumn. She has always held a special place in my heart. She has her Father's (and mine) sense of humor. She is very caring and tries to never hurt anyone's feelings. She is truly an Angel set right from above for all of us to love. She has brightened my life in ways I could never hope to explain.

I LOVE YOU, AUTUMN!

And notice I did not forget the N.

AUTUMN

The very word brings to mind changes as everything must change

It happens to be my Granddaughter's name, and she does the same

There are many things she has brought to my life; the most important is joy

I haven't been able to spend much time with her, the times I have, I so enjoy

She just touches my heart in ways I just can't even start to explain

I so desperately want to connect with her and have her feel the same

She managed, somehow, to soften this once tough, hardened Marine Heart

She did this with her warm smile and quiet, loving way right from the start

I want to express my love and tell her how I feel within the confines of this poem

There is a special place for her within this heart of mine, in which will always be her home.

I LOVE YOU, AUTUMN!

William Arthur Nahmens

XANDER, MY GRANDSON
About the Poem

I wrote "He's My Grandson" for my Grandson Xander. I only see him once a year, but I still feel we have bonded somehow. When I am no longer able to travel or see him anymore, my greatest wish is that he will remember Grandpa Nahmens and know the joy he brought into my life and how much I loved him. I know my Daughter Sarah (Xander's Mother) will never let me slip from his memory.

HE'S MY GRANDSON

He is my Grandson; his name is Xander, he is quite the little man,

I am so glad I got the chance to see him; after all, I am his biggest fan.

His ways and words will sometimes make you forget his young age,

Every day I spend with him is like turning a book to a new page.

Each day, there is something new that makes me scratch my head,

Something new he has done, or maybe it was something he said.

His energy level is always high and seems to have no end,

He wears me out fast; I wish he had some of his to lend.

My biggest hope is that he will always remember Grandpa's love,

Long after the time I have left to go to my home above.

ALWAYS REMEMBER, XANDER, GRANPA LOVES YOU!

William Arthur Nahmens

MY EMMA GENE
About the Poem

    I wrote this poem as a message to my Granddaughter, Emma Gene. I knew my time with her would be short, so I wanted to tell her that no matter what, I would come from wherever I may be to protect her. I also wanted it to serve as a warning to anyone who hurts her in any way. Above all, I want her to know, feel, and always remember how much her Grandpa Nahmens loved her.

MY EMMA GENE

She is my Granddaughter, her name is Emma Gene,

Her demeanor reminds me of her Mother, Sarah Gene.

Her very light blonde hair and deep blue eyes take me back,

From a time when Sarah was small, her love for me had no lack

I find myself with the same feelings as I look into those eyes,

I get the feeling that my heart is breaking every time she cries.

Little girls are so much different than little boys, you know,

Something about little girls, there's a need to protect them more.

I make this promise to my Emma, if she ever needs me, just yell,

I will do whatever it takes to get to her, moving heaven and hell.

To protect her from danger, I will be there to pull her from the fire.

This she can believe and count on; Grandpa will always be beside her.

I am peaceful, I am not a violent man, but I can get mad dog mean,

Heaven help any living thing that ever hurts my sweet Emma Gene!

I LOVE YOU! MY SWEET LITTLE EMMA GENE

William Arthur Nahmens

TO KYLIE
About the Poem

I wrote "To Kylie" (who is actually my 3rd Cousin) for her
Birthday. She was no longer a "child," but a young woman, Yet I
could not see her as anything more than a child. She always calls
me "Uncle Bill" even though I am not her Uncle; this show of
respect has always touched my heart. I remember when I first
moved back to Wisconsin. We always went on a family trip to the
Dells. She was probably only 3 or 4 then; she would stand by the
side of the pool and jump into my arms or go down a water slide,
and I would catch her. It reminded me so much of the times
when my daughter Sarah would jump (ever trustingly) into my
arms. As I watched her grow, I watched her endure Heartaches
that could make any child bitter. She has always retained her
sweet spirit. I tease her a lot (as if she were still a little kid), but
it is out of a heartfelt sense of gratitude. This little girl melted my
cold, hard heart with the warmth and love she showed to
everyone.

TO KYLIE

From "Uncle Bill"

Your smile can melt the coldest of hearts

Your tears can break the hardest ones apart

You have a sweet innocence that flows from your soul

So difficult to accept you are no longer a child but 19 years old

The love and kindness you show towards others is something
untaught

It was learned through heartaches and life's battles you have already
fought.

You have an inner strength and beauty that you may not be aware of

It's there! It abounds, rising from your sweet spirit much like a dove

You call me "Uncle Bill" even though we both know I am just a cousin

The honor I feel when you say that melts this heart; I thought it was
hardened

You really are the kindest, gentlest, most caring person I know.

I know I tease you a lot, but in this poem, my true feelings I show.

HAPPY BIRTHDAY, KYLIE!

Wilm Arthur Nahmens

TO ALICE
About the Poem

I had a very close friend growing up; her name Alice Ringer. She was my first friend when my family moved from New Berlin, Wisconsin, to Muskego, Wisconsin, in the early 1960s. We became very close during those early years. I was either at her house or she was at mine. She knew the hardships I went through in my early life. She watched as I turned into a troubled Teenager. As I grew older, we drifted apart. When my family moved from the neighborhood, we hardly spoke anymore., even though I still saw her at school. The last time was during Graduation in June of 1973. I often thought of her over the years. In June of 2023, I attended my 50th Class reunion. Alice was there. Although we had commented on posts on Facebook, we still hadn't spoken. At the reunion, we started talking. It felt like we had never lost touch with each other. We picked up right where we left off over 50 years later. It felt good, and I did not want it to end. A few days later, I learned it was her Birthday. I sat and wrote this poem "To Alice" (I originally titled "For Alice"). As I wrote, all my feelings for her started to surface, and I discovered (within myself) that she was actually my first love (although I didn't understand it way back then). She has always held a special place in my heart.

TO ALICE

My childhood friend

You were always a very close friend

Never giving up on me, even to the end

No one knew the hell I was going through

No one, that is, except for one, that was you!

I never realized it, but you were my first love

You were always there that I could be sure of

For years, I felt so lost as we drifted apart

You always held a special place in my heart.

Words I should have said but were never spoken

Things I wished I had told you had left my heart broken

I was too afraid to admit how much you meant to me

The deep feelings I held for you, I was just too blind to see.

Over the years, oftentimes, I would think of you, holding on to a small part.

I moved away from my childhood friend, but you never moved from my heart.

William Arthur Nahmens

TO ARNEETRICE
About the Poem

I wrote "Io Arneetrice" the day she told me she was retiring by the end of the year. She said she wanted to tell me first as she felt we shared a "special bond." I wanted to tell her how much she helped me through one of the most difficult periods of my life (the loss of most of my eyesight). I wanted her to know that even though I know life will go on, she will be missed and never forgotten. She has given hope to many Veterans, reaching them in her own special way. She is one of those special Souls that come along only once in a lifetime.

THANK YOU ARNEETRICE!

TO ARNEETRICE
GO WITH OUR LOVE

As you begin your new life, you take with you all of our love

You've lit the pathway for many Veterans along their weary way

You have helped each one of us, much like an Angel sent from above

Always there to lead us through the darkness and find the light of day

You will not be forgotten; you will be missed by all of us; you see

You have reached all of us, giving each hope where once there was none

of all those you've touched, I feel you have touched none as deeply as me

You made a difference to many, but none were changed more than this one

My heart and soul were lost deep in the darkness; I had no hope, no will to go on.

You talked me through, but more, you listened while wiping my hidden tears away.

By sharing your own struggles and heartaches, we formed an unbreakable bond.

Even though I know I can make it and, I'll be ok. I will miss you, Arneetrice Gray.

William Arthur Nahmens

THE DAY YOUR COUNTRY CALLED
About the Poem

I wrote "The Day Your Country Called" For a very special Brother-in -
Arms. Although I am not a combat Veteran, I have always felt a special
kinship with him. The original poem was lost when my computer
crashed before backing it up, so I rewrote it from memory. While the
words are not exactly the same, the sentient is! I rewrote the poem
again and dedicated it to those who did not make it back and whose
names are on "The Wall."

THE DAY YOUR COUNTRY CALLED

The day your country called,

You were there to answer the call

Not sure of what the future did hold

Not sure if you would ever grow old.

You left your home for some faraway land

You left to risk your life on foreign sand!

Each and every day, with every single breath

For others, you fought, facing certain death.

Your blood was spilled upon foreign ground

But still, you got up; you wouldn't stay down.

When you left, you left behind part of your soul

No one bit you can ever know how heavy the toll

For your eyes have seen things others have not

And your soul has bled in ways others cannot

I thank God your name is **not** on "the wall."

And thank you for you answered the call.

William Arthur Nahmens

PART TWO

A FEW FROM THE HIP

A collection of Humorous stories I have told over the years and my collection of "Bad Dad Jokes."

"FOOD FOR THOUGHT"

I'm 69 years old, and I have realized I still have so many unanswered questions! I never found out who let the dogs out... the way to get to Sesame Street... why Dora doesn't just use Google Maps... why "abbreviated" is such a long word... why lemonade is made with artificial flavor yet dish-washing liquid is made with real lemons... why they sterilize the needle for lethal injections... and, why do you have to "put your two cents in" but it's only a "penny for your thoughts" where's that extra penny going to... why do The Alphabet Song and Twinkle Twinkle Little Star have the same tune... why did you just try to sing those two previous songs... and just what is Victoria's secret? Spoiler Alert: Victoria's Secret is owned & RAN by a MAN, always has ...and do you really think I am this witty ?? ... I actually stole this from a friend who stole it from a friend of her brother's girlfriend's uncle's cousin's, baby mamma's doctor...Now it is your turn to steal it from me...

"THE MORAL OF THE STORY IS"

These next few pages contain some of the stories I have used in the past as sort of a teaching moment. They are humorous but still carry a message.

THE DEFIANT ROBIN
About the Story

I first used this story when I was a Marine Sergeant. My Troops were complaining about Military life and how much they hated it. I would tell them this story and then say: "Are you warm and happy? Then shut up!" I do not know who wrote it, but it sure fits life. The original story used a sparrow; I changed it to a Robin as Sparrows do not migrate.

THE DEFIANT ROBIN

One Fall, a Robin decided not to fly south for the winter. All the other Robins told him he was stupid. They said, "If you stay here, you will die!" The defiant little Robin asked, "How do you know? Have any of you ever stayed behind to find out what happens?" As fall went on, all the other Robins headed south. The defiant Robin (confident in his decision) stayed behind. Soon, winter hit! The defiant Robin got very cold and decided he should head south after all! As he was flying, his wings iced up, and he crashed headlong into a Farmer's field! Laying, freezing, he thought to himself, "Why was I so defiant! Now I am going to freeze to death and die all alone in this field!" About that time, a cow came walking along and shit right on the poor Robin. "That's just great!" The robin said to himself, "Here I am dying, and someone takes a shit on me!" Soon, Robin found that the manure was warm, and he started to thaw out. Feeling warm and happy, the little bird started singing. At that time, a cat came walking by, heard the singing, dug through the manure, found the bird, and promptly ate him!

What three lessons do we learn from this story?

1. Just because someone shits on you, it doesn't necessarily mean they are your enemy.

2. Just because someone digs you out of the shit, it doesn't necessarily mean they are your friend.

3. AND if you are warm and happy in a pile of shit:

   KEEP YOUR MOUTH SHUT!

THE HUNGRY HORSEFLY
About the Story

I told this story the first time to my Platoon when I was a Sergeant in the Marines. It was at a time when a lot of them were ranting and raving about something they really knew nothing about. Years later, I told it to my second wife when she was yelling at me about something I had nothing to do with. Before I told her "The Moral of the Story," She looked at me with this "I don't get it, why are you telling me this in the middle of a fight" look, then there was a moment of anger from her, and then we were both laughing about the whole thing.

THE HUNGRY HORSEFLY

One day, there was this very hungry horsefly who happened upon an old barn that was full of manure. The barn was undiscovered by other flies. The Horsefly thought to himself, "This is great! The whole barn is mine and mine alone!" The fly started eating, and he ate and ate until his belly was ready to burst, and he couldn't eat anymore. He decided it was time to leave (thinking he would return in a day or two to eat some more). He tried to take off but was too heavy to get off the ground. He took a running start and jumped up but just fell to the ground again. Looking around, he spied a pitchfork leaning against the wall in a corner. He climbed up the pitchfork to the top of the handle and jumped off. He immediately fell to the ground, hitting it with a splat, and died.

AND THE MORAL IS

Are you ready for this?

DON'T GO FLYING OFF THE HANDLE

IF YOU'RE FULL OF SHIT!

WHO IS THE BOSS?

About the Story

I heard this many years ago (early in my Marine Corps days). I don't know where it originated from. After I became a Sergeant, I would occasionally run into an Officer (usually a 2nd Lieutenant) who was just a total ass because of his rank. I would tell the men in my Platoon this story, and after hearing it, they would just bust out laughing every time the 2nd Lieutenant came around. The 2nd lieuy never understood why. I used it in the civilian world whenever I would run into a boss who was just a total ass. I hope it amuses here.

WHO IS THE BOSS?

When god first created man, a debate broke out over which part of the body should be the boss.

The brain argued that since he did all the thinking for the man, he should be the boss.

The eyes reasoned that since they could see where the man was going, they should be the boss since, without them, the man would surely fall off a cliff and die.

The arms and hands were next arguing that, without them, the main could not build tools, and without such tools, the man would surely die.

The legs applied for the job, arguing that since only they could take the man wherever he needed to go, they should be the boss.

And so it went, with each part of the body explaining why they should be the boss. Then one day, the lowly asshole applied for the job. The other parts of the body laughed so hard that the asshole closed up and refused to function. In three days, the brain was foggy, and could not think straight; the eyes were crossed and could not focus; the arms and hands hung helplessly at the man's sides. The legs were shakey and weak, and could not hold the man up. All agreed to let the asshole be the boss, except the brain he alone was holding out, insisting he should be the boss. After a week, the brain finally relented and let the asshole be the boss.

WHICH JUST GOES TO PROVE:

YOU DON'T HAVE TO BE A BRAIN TO BE A BOSS, JUST AN ASSHOLE!

THE OLD MAN AND THE LAWYER
About the Story

I don't know when I first heard this story or even where it came from. I have told this story several times to younger people over the years. I first told it when a teenager was making comments about my inability to work my iPhone. I didn't know how to text, get apps, or even use a tablet. They would ask me tech questions that they were pretty sure I did not know the answers to. So, I would give them questions that called for common sense. I would then (after they gave up trying to answer my question) tell them this story. I don't know if they understood the meaning, but they sure were quick to point out that the old man (in their opinion) cheated.

THE OLD MAN AND THE LAWYER

While waiting for his plane to take off, a young lawyer was surfing the web on his tablet and using his iPhone to get the current news from around the world; sitting next to him was an old man struggling to read a day-old newspaper. The young lawyer, believing old people are dumb and way behind times, decided he could get one over on the old man and maybe make an easy buck. So, the lawyer asks the old man if he would like to play a game. The old man says he is tired and just wants to take a nap; folding up his newspaper, he politely declines and tries to catch a few winks. The lawyer persists and says that the game is easy and a lot of fun. "I ask you a question, and if you don't know the answer, you pay me just $5.00, then you ask me a question, and if I can't find the answer, I will pay you $500!" This catches the old man's attention, and so he agrees to play the game. The lawyer asks the first question. 'What's the distance from The Earth to the Moon?' The old man doesn't say a word; he just reaches into his pocket, pulls out a five-dollar bill, and hands it to the lawyer. "Now," the lawyer says, "it's your turn. What is your question?" The old man, thinking for a minute, asks the lawyer, 'What goes up a hill with three legs in the morning but comes down with four legs at night?' The lawyer uses his laptop and searches all the references he can find on the Net. He sends e-mails to his smartest friends, all to no avail. After more than an hour of searching, he finally gives up. He wakes up the old man and hands him $500. The old man pockets the $500 and goes right back to sleep. The lawyer is going nuts, not knowing the answer. He wakes the old man up and asks, 'Well? What does go up a hill with three legs in the morning and comes down with four at night?' Without saying a word, the old man reaches into his pocket, hands the lawyer a $5 bill, and goes back to sleep.

The Moral of the Story:

**DON'T MESS WITH OLD PEOPLE,
YOU MAY HAVE BOOK SMARTS, BUT WE HAVE WISDOM, AND YOU
CANNOT LEARN WISDOM FROM A BOOK; IT TAKES A LIFETIME OF
LIFE'S HARD KNOCKS TO LEARN IT!**

BUT YOU COULD HAVE

About the Story

I stumbled across this story while looking for something about paying for something that you never used. The Author is anonymous, but it really made me laugh when I thought of all the amenities you pay for at a Hotel/Motel without ever using them; I hope you find it as numerous as I did!

BUT YOU COULD HAVE

A woman decided to give herself a big treat for her 70th birthday by staying overnight in a really nice hotel. When she checked out the next morning, the desk clerk handed her a bill for $250.00. She demanded to know why the charge was so high. "I agree it's a nice hotel, but the rooms aren't worth $250.00 for just an overnight stay - I didn't even have breakfast!" The clerk told her that $250.00 was the 'standard rate,' and breakfast had been included had she wanted it.

She insisted on speaking to the Manager. The Manager appeared and, forewarned by the desk clerk, announced: "This hotel has an Olympic-sized pool and a huge conference center, which are available for use." "But I didn't use them." 'Well, they are here, and you could have.' He went on to explain that she could also have seen one of the in-hotel shows for which they were so famous. "We have the best entertainers from the world over performing here." "But I didn't go to any of those shows." "Well, we have them, and you could have." No matter what amenity the Manager mentioned, she replied, "But I didn't use it!" and the Manager countered with his standard response. After several minutes of discussion, and with the Manager still unmoved, she decided to pay, wrote a check, and gave it to him. The Manager was surprised when he looked at the check. "But, Madam, this check is for only $50.00." "That's correct; I charged you $200.00 for sleeping with me." "But I didn't!" "Well, too bad, I was here, and you could have."

And The Moral Is:

LIFE IS FULL OF COULD HAVES BUT DIDN'TS!

HUMOROUS STORIES

I have told over the years.

IS THERE SUCH A THING AS AN HONEST POLITICIAN?

I often think about this and wonder what the answer is. My belief is that the words "honest" and "Politician" should never be used in the same breath as they do not fit together. To prove my point, I offer the following (almost true) story.

My Grandfather and I were walking through a cemetery on our way to visit my Grandmother's grave. As we walked past a newly marked grave, my Grandfather read the tombstone. It read, "Here lies a politician and an honest man." My Grandfather, shaking his head slowly, said to me, "Isn't it a shame, Billy? They had to bury two fellas in the same hole!"

I ONCE WAS A MONK

A lot of people don't know this about me, but I was once a Monk. I did this for fifteen years. It was very difficult for me as we had to take a vow of silence, which (as anyone who knows me will tell you) would be all but almost impossible for me to keep. Every five years, we all gathered in the large meeting room where each of us could speak two, and ONLY two, words, no more! After the first five years had passed, when it was my turn, I said, "Food bad." After the next five years, I said, "bed, hard!" Finally, five long more years passed, and I said, "I quit!"

JUST CALL ME BUBBA

A man boarded an airplane and took his seat. As he settled in, he glanced up and saw the most beautiful woman he'd ever seen boarding the plane. He soon realized She was heading straight towards his seat. As fate would have it, she took the seat right beside his:

Eager to strike up a conversation, he blurted out. "Business trip or pleasure?"

She turned, smiled and said. "Business. I'm going to the Annual Sex Symposium of America in Boston."

He swallowed hard. Here was the most gorgeous woman he had ever seen. Sitting next to him, and she was going to a Sex Symposium!

Struggling to maintain his composure, he calmly asked. "What's your Business at this Symposium?"

"Lecturer." She responded. "I use information that I have learned from my Personal experiences to debunk some of the popular myths about sexuality."

"Really?" He said. "And what kind of myths are they?"

"Well." She explained. "One popular myth is that African-American men are The most well-endowed of all men, when in fact, it is the Native American Indian who is most likely to possess that trait. Another popular myth is That Frenchmen are the best lovers when, actually, it is men of Mexican Descent who are the best. I have also discovered that the lover with Absolutely the best stamina is the Southern Redneck."

Suddenly, the woman became a little uncomfortable and blushed. "I'm Sorry." She said, "I shouldn't really be discussing all of this with you. I don't even know your name."

"Tonto." The man said. "Tonto Gonzales, but my friends back home just call me Bubba."

THE BARBER

One day, a florist went into a barber shop for a haircut. After the haircut was over, the florist asked the barber for his bill. "I cannot accept any money," the Barber replied, "I am doing community service this week." The florist told the barber how pleased he was with a haircut and left the shop.

The next day, when the barber arrived at his shop, there were a dozen roses at his door with a thank you note waiting for him. Later that same day, a Cop entered the barber shop and asked for a haircut. After the haircut, the cop expressed his delight with the haircut and tried to hand the barber thirty dollars. Once again, the barber replied, "I am doing Community Service this week, so no money is required." The cop thanked the barber for the haircut and left the shop.

The next day, when the barber arrived at his shop, there were a dozen doughnuts and a thank you note waiting for him. Later that day, a Congressman entered the shop and asked for a haircut. When the Congressman asked how much he owed, the barber once again replied, "I am doing community service this week, so there is no charge." The Congressman thanked the barber and left.

The next day, when the barber arrived at his shop, there were a dozen members of Congress lined up waiting for their free haircut. They also presented the barber shop owner with a Tax bill for the gifts he had received for his services.

AND THAT MY FRIENDS IS THE DIFFERENCE BETWEEN:

THE CITIZENS OF OUR COUNTRY

AND THE POLITICIANS WHO RUN IT

These next pages contain some of my best (or worst, depending on how you look at it) Dad/Grandpa jokes.

****

A big moron and a little more on we standing at the top of a cliff,

The big moron fell off; why didn't the little moron?

Because he was a little more on!

****

There once was a family named Bigger:

Baby Bigger, Mama Bigger, and Daddy Bigger.

Which was the biggest?

Baby Bigger. He was just a little Bigger!

****

What animal can you never trust?

A Lion, because he is always a lion

****

What did the daddy buffalo say to his son when he dropped him off at school?

"Bye son!"

****

What animal never wears shoes?

A bear! (he is always bear-footed).

****

Why can't bicycles stand up?

Because they are just too tired!

****

What gets bigger the more you take away from it?

A hole!

****

Why do Elephants wear green tennis shoes?

So they can hide in trees.

***

Ever seen an elephant in a tree?

They hide pretty good, don't they!

****

Why was the elephant wearing red tennis shoes?

Because his green ones were in the wash!

******

Why do you never go into the jungle after 4:30 at night?

Because that's when the elephants are jumping out of the trees!

****

Why are crocodiles flat?

Because they went into the jungle after 4:30 at night!

****

What is black and white and read all over?

A newspaper!

*****

What is black and white and red all over?

A Zebra with a sunburn

****

What is Black and white and red all over?

A skunk with a diaper rash!

****

What is green and grows and rolls on wheels?

Grass! (I lied about the wheels).

****

What time is it when you go to the Dentist?

Tooth-Hurty

****

What has two hands but no arms?

A clock

****

My Dad used to have a job in a clock factory

He just stood around all day, making faces

ALWAYS REMEMBER...LAUGHTER IS THE BEST MEDICINE FOR A WEARY SOUL...

IN CLOSING, I OFFER THIS ONE LAST THOUGHT:

I found the following on the net. I do not know who wrote it; it was part of a longer story. It moved me so much that I decided to end my book with it.

I WISH YOU ENOUGH

I wish you enough sun to keep your attitude bright no matter how gray the day may appear,
I wish you enough rain to appreciate the sun even more.

I wish you enough happiness to keep your spirit alive and everlasting;
I wish you enough pain so that even the smallest of joys in life may appear bigger.

I wish you enough gain to satisfy your wants,
I wish you enough loss to appreciate all that you possess.

I wish you enough hellos,
to get you through the final goodbye.

Thanks for allowing me to share my heart and soul with you
I hope you enjoyed the Ramblings of this old man

THE END*

William Arthur Nahmens

Well maybe

Milton Keynes UK
Ingram Content Group UK Ltd.
UKRC032145201123
432958UK00007B/148

* 9 7 9 8 8 6 8 9 8 1 8 8 3 *